TOP 25

GYMNASTICS

SKILLS, TIPS, AND TRICKS

JEFF SAVAGE

Enslow Publishers, Inc.
40 Industrial Road
Box 398
Berkeley Heights, NJ 07922
USA

http://www.enslow.com

Library of Congress Cataloging-in-Publication Data

Savage, Jeff, 1961–
   Top 25 gymnastics skills, tips, and tricks / Jeff Savage.
       p. cm. — (Top 25 sports skills, tips, and tricks)
   Includes index.
   Summary: "Examines gymnastics skills, including techniques for the floor exercise, vault, bars, rings, balance beam, and
pommel horse, and provides tips and tricks for young, aspiring gymnasts"—Provided by publisher.
   ISBN 978-0-7660-3868-4 (library bound) — ISBN 978-1-59845-358-4 (pbk.)
   1. Gymnastics—Training—Juvenile literature. I. Title. II. Title: Top twenty-five gymnastics skills, tips, and tricks.
   GV461.3.S28 2012
   796.44—dc22
                                          2011011338

Paperback ISBN 978-1-59845-358-4

Printed in the United States of America

062011 Lake Book Manufacturing, Inc., Melrose Park, IL

10 9 8 7 6 5 4 3 2 1

Do not attempt the more advanced skills and tricks without adult supervision.

To Our Readers:
We have done our best to make sure all Internet addresses in this book were active and appropriate when we went to press.
However, the author and the publisher have no control over and assume no liability for the material available on those Internet
sites or on other Web sites they may link to. Any comments or suggestions can be sent by e-mail to comments@enslow.com or
to the address on the back cover.

♻ Enslow Publishers, Inc., is committed to printing our books on recycled paper. The paper in every book contains 10% to
30% post-consumer waste (PCW). The cover board on the outside of each book contains 100% PCW. Our goal is to do our part
to help young people and the environment too!

Illustration Credits: AP Images / Ed Reinke, p. 15; AP Images / Jamie Schwaberow, p. 19 (right); AP Images / Julie
Jacobson, p. 29; AP Images / Matt Dunham, p. 45; AP Images / Matt Marriott / NCAA Photos, p. 30; AP Images / Ng Han
Guan, p. 6; AP Images / Rick Rycroft, p. 31; AP Images / Rob Carr, p. 23; John Cheng / Team Photo, pp. 4, 5, 9, 11, 13, 17,
20, 21, 22, 33, 35, 37, 39, 41, 43; © PCN Photography / Alamy, p. 1; Shutterstock.com, pp. 7, 14, 19 (left), 25, 27, 32, 36,
42, 44.

Cover Illustration: © PCN Photography / Alamy (Young gymnast on the balance beam).

CONTENTS

INTRODUCTION

Gymnastics is a sport of tricks.

Gymnasts at the highest level perform breathtaking spins and flips. We marvel at the strength and agility of these elite athletes. To reach this point, gymnasts spend years practicing. They start with basic skills. They perfect each skill before advancing to the next skill level. These are called progressions. For instance, it might take years for a gymnast to progress from a handstand, to a walkover, to a back handspring. Smart gymnasts know they must repeat each trick over and over again until they get it right every time. Patience is the key.

Women's artistic gymnastics features four events. The men's competition has six. Two of the events are the same—floor exercise and vault. In all events, judges score each gymnast's performance.

A young gymnast practices on the balance beam with her coach. To reach the elite level of gymnastics, it takes years of practice and hard work.

Elite level gymnasts perform amazing skills and tricks with flawless technique. But elite level gymnasts do not achieve success overnight. They advance skill level by skill level until they are performing remarkable flips and spins.

ON THE FLOOR

Floor exercise takes place on a square-shaped padded floor about forty feet wide. Gymnasts perform tumbling passes to demonstrate balance, agility, and grace.

1 BODY SHAPES

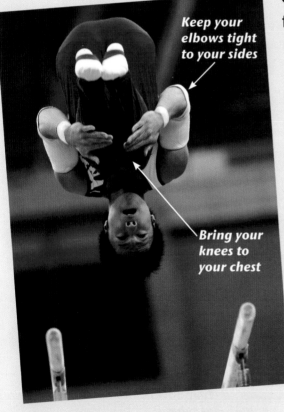

Keep your elbows tight to your sides

Bring your knees to your chest

On the floor, you should be able to form several shapes with your body. Here are seven basic shapes that you should know.

1. **Straight**—To stand straight, hold your body tight by squeezing your muscles. This is called body tension. Hold your arms to your sides. Pretend you are a pencil.

2. **Basic Pike**—Keep your upper and lower body straight. Bend at the waist to form a 90-degree angle. Hold your arms out straight.

3. **Closed Pike**—Lean farther than the basic pike so that your upper body closes down parallel to your lower body. Extend your arms toward your feet.

Japanese gymnast Kyoichi Watanabe turns in the air in the tuck position during a routine on the parallel bars at the Asian Games in China.

4. **Tuck**—Bend at your waist. Draw your knees to your chest. Keep your elbows tight to your sides.

5. **Hollow**—Lay on your back. Raise your head and feet up slightly. Extend your arms to your knees. Your body is now in the shape of a curved dish.

6. **Arch**—Lay on your stomach. Straighten your arms and legs. Raise them up high.

7. **Bridge**—Lay on your back. Place your feet flat on the floor. Bend your arms and place your hands by your ears, palms flat on the floor. Rise up on your hands and feet. Your stomach should be your highest point. Your body should form an arch.

Arch your back

Palms and feet should be flat on the floor

This young gymnast displays the bridge position.

2 BALANCING

Balance is the ability to hold your position or change positions while maintaining control. Having good balance requires using your center of gravity. As you form different shapes, you want to keep this point "centered" over your base of support.

Practice standing in several basic positions. Stand with your feet shoulder-width apart and keep your head still while looking straight ahead. Now change the position of your arms. Extend your arms straight out to the sides. Hold one arm straight down and the other straight up over your head. Hold one arm across your chest and the other straight to the same side. Hold both arms straight up and lift up on your toes.

Stand only on one foot. Keep both legs straight by locking them at the knees. Raise one leg slightly forward with your toes pointed. Pull your leg back and slightly to the side. Try using different arm positions as you did standing on both feet.

Advanced balancing moves on one leg for girls are called arabesques. For boys they are called scales. Girls also do scales. Many of these moves involve bending sideways while extending the opposite leg out or up. For instance, to perform a Y-scale, you should be able to stand on one leg and bring your other leg all the way up to your head without bending it.

Another difficult balancing act is performing a headstand. Put your hands on the floor well in front of your knees. Place your forehead on the floor in front of your hands. Make a triangle between your head and hands. Carefully move forward and rise up on your toes while keeping your knees bent. Lift one leg behind you. Use your head and hands as your three points of pressure. Lift your other leg behind you. Straighten your legs.

A handstand can be even trickier. Put your hands on the floor with your arms straight. Try to kick your legs up in the air. To practice, lean your back against a wall for support.

It is important to develop good balance in several basic positions before advancing to more complicated skills. However, as you learn, you can push yourself to try more difficult skills. With the assistance of a coach, this gymnast practices a handstand. Practice this tricky skill against a wall or with a coach's help.

3 ROLLING

Rolling is another floor exercise. Simple rolls are building blocks to more difficult rolls. Two of the simplest are the forward roll and backward roll.

To start the forward roll, lie on your back in the tuck position. Rock yourself backward to your shoulders then forward to your feet. Rocking back and forth this way will give you a good sense of rolling. Next, increase the power of the roll until you can rise up on your feet. To get extra momentum, extend your arms forward. Once you feel comfortable getting to your feet, you are ready to start from a standing position. Crouch into a tuck and place your hands on the floor in front of your feet. Tuck your chin to your chest. Push off your feet. Roll upside down onto your back. Rise to your feet.

The backward roll is trickier. Sit on the floor in the tuck position as you would for the forward roll. But instead of placing your hands on your knees, this time put them by the sides of your head with palms up like you're holding a pizza. Point your elbows forward. Keep your chin to your chest. Rock back and forth to get the feel of it. Now, roll backward with enough force that your hips rise above your shoulders. Put your hands onto the floor. Do not roll on your head. Straighten your arms and push off the floor. Your legs should swing over until your feet touch the floor. Keep your balance and stand up. When you think it is safe, you can try the roll from a standing position.

Forward and backward rolls can start or finish in the straddle stand. Straddling is keeping your legs straight and wider than shoulder width.

Rolling is another aspect of the floor exercise, and the forward roll is the most basic roll. As a beginner, it helps to practice rocking yourself on your back until you get comfortable. After a lot of practice, you will be able to begin a forward roll standing up.

4 ACROBATICS

A thrilling part of floor exercise is doing stunts in the air. These are called acrobatics. Most acrobatics come from two basic moves—the cartwheel and the handspring. A strong handstand is a prerequisite to a cartwheel and a good handspring.

To perform a cartwheel, stand on one leg with your arms high. Lean over until your leading leg (the leg that starts in the air) and one hand touch the floor. Remember to look down at where you are going. Push hard off your leading leg. Your second hand should touch the floor as your trailing leg rises. You are now in a handstand! Keep your legs wide. If you have kicked hard enough, your momentum will keep you going. Touch the floor with your leading leg and bend it to absorb your weight and force. Continue rotating with your arms wide. Touch the floor with your trailing leg and finish in a straddle stand. A round off starts like a cartwheel. But at the top, put your feet together. Land facing the direction you came from.

A handspring is a flip from the feet to the hands and back to the feet again. To perform a front or back handspring, ask your coach or instructor.

THEN AND NOW

Men's gymnastics was part of the first modern Olympics in 1896. Events included running, high jumping, and climbing a twenty-foot-long rope. Men's exercises today are vault, parallel bars, pommel horse, floor exercise, still rings, and high bar.

A cartwheel is a basic acrobatic move. Make sure to look down to see where you are going. At the top of the move, you should be completely upside down with your feet apart. Practice perfecting your handstand and that will help you get better at cartwheels.

5 PUTTING IT TOGETHER

A floor routine is the art of combining shapes and balances with rolls and acrobatics. A routine lasts between sixty and ninety seconds. In that time, a gymnast performs at least three tricky combinations called tumbling passes. The passes are linked together with one-foot pivots and other turns and jumps. For girls, these are called dance elements.

You want to use dynamic flips and twists that reflect your personality. Your routine should demonstrate both power and grace. At its best, it should feature daring moves under control. Girls generally perform floor exercise to music and boys do not.

Tumbling passes are the most exciting part of the floor exercise. During these passes, gymnasts perform dynamic flips and twists. This is the most difficult part of the floor exercise to master, and it requires many years of practice.

DID YOU KNOW?

Gymnastics originated in ancient Greece. Physical activity was important. Only male athletes were allowed to compete.

PRO TIPS AND TRICKS

Shannon Miller is America's most decorated gymnast. She won seven Olympic and nine World Championship medals. Miller sees gymnastics as a challenge. "In gymnastics, the longest routine you do is a minute and a half, and that's pretty tough to get through," she says. "You have to be perfect every step along the way. Gymnastics uses every single part of your body, every little tiny muscle that you never even knew."

Shannon Miller performs her routine in the floor exercise at the 1996 Olympic Games in Atlanta, Georgia.

VAULTING IN THE AIR

Vault is the other event in which both men and women compete. It is performed using two apparatus, a springboard and a vaulting table. Gymnasts sprint down a runway, jump onto the springboard, propel hands-first onto the table, and land on their feet. This exciting event is over in a matter of seconds.

 RUN-UP

In elite competitions, a runway is eighty-two feet long. You can start your run-up to the springboard at any point on the runway. The farther back you start, the better. Why? Because you want to run as fast as you can to build momentum. Speed generates power. You want to hit the springboard with as much force as possible.

Your run should be even and direct. Thrust hard with your legs. Raise your knees high. Pump your arms, but do not let them go across the front of you. Instead, turn your palms up slightly. Keep your arms bent. As you run, accelerate. The best way to improve your speed is to run sprints.

A few feet from the springboard is your hurdle point. The hurdle is a long, low jump from one foot to two feet.

The run-up to the springboard is the first part of the vault event. You want to create as much momentum as possible during your run-up.

Pump your arms and keep your palms up slightly.

Be sure to keep your hurdle long and low to the ground. The board is built to transfer forward momentum upward. You want to hurdle more into the board, rather than onto the board.

Raise your knees high

DID YOU KNOW?

In the vault competition, if a female athlete stops during her run before she touches the springboard, she is given a second chance. Male gymnasts must complete their attempt on the first try.

7 PREFLIGHT

The springboard measures two feet by four feet with thick springs inside. Upon contact, your body should be leaning back slightly. Extend your feet so that they are in front of your hips. If you are vertical or leaning forward, you could smack face-first into the vault table.

To do a handspring vault, raise your arms so that they are tight against your ears. Punch the springboard hard off your heels. Explode off the board. Keep your legs together and straight. Point your toes down. Keep your body tight. Focus your eyes on the table.

There are more complex vaults. A half-on entry is a handspring combined with a half-turn, like a round off. To turn, do not throw a shoulder forward. Instead, pull a shoulder back. This helps keep your posture straight. Do not twist too early. Higher level gymnasts perform trickier vaults. A Tsukahara-style vault involves a ¼–½ turn in preflight. A Yurchenko-style vault involves a round off back handspring so that you are facing away from the vault table upon contact. Do not attempt advanced elements without supervision. It is unsafe to be confused in the air.

PRO TIPS AND TRICKS

In 1984, American Mary Lou Retton became the first female gymnast outside Eastern Europe to win the Olympic all-around gold medal. Retton says success on the vault starts with a strong run. "If you want to be a good vaulter, you can't slow down when you're running to the board," she says. "Don't be afraid. Just make sure your steps are right and go for it!"

One of the basic vaults is the handspring vault. With any vault, make sure to explode off the board and keep your eyes on the table.

Raise your arms tight against your ears for the handspring vault.

The springboard and vault table

Hit the springboard with your heels

CONTACT

The vault table is like a padded box. It is four feet long and three feet wide. Its height varies around four feet. Gymnasts push off the table from their hands with as much as five hundred pounds of pressure per square inch. This is called blocking.

To block correctly, focus directly at the point of contact. Your body should be straight, nearly in the hollow position. Your arms should be extended and firm. You should make contact when you are completely upside down. Push the table with your hands. Extend your shoulders into the table like a shoulder shrug, as though you are pushing the table down. Use as much force as possible to propel into the air.

Pushing off the table is called blocking. You must block properly to propel yourself into the air.

9 IN THE AIR

The second airborne stage of vault is traveling from the table to the floor. This is sometimes referred to as postflight, though you are actually in flight. It involves flips and twists and is generally considered the most exciting part of the exercise.

Elite vaulters go as high as eight feet in the air. The higher you are, the more tricks you can do. Nearly all involve some variation of the somersault. A somersault simply means moving your feet over your head—a 360-degree flip. A somersault can be forward, backward, or sideways. You can include a ¼ turn, ½ turn, full turn, or more. You can perform a back somersault with 1½ twists, a front somersault to a back landing, and so on.

In the tuck position, pull your chin to your chest so that you are looking at your belly button. In the hollow position, keep your head straight and your body hollow. For the pike position, you bend at the waist. Your legs should be straight and together. In both positions, keep your toes pointed.

JANSSEN·FRITSEN

The second stage of vault, or postflight, is the most exciting part of the exercise. Elite vaulters soar as high as eight feet in the air allowing them to do multiple twists and turns.

10 LANDING

No matter how many twists and flips you do, your top priority is to land safely. Elite gymnasts must land in a specific area marked by boundary lines.

As you land, extend your arms in front and slightly out to your sides. Hold your feet a few inches apart. Point your toes out a bit. Most important, bend your knees slightly. This will soften the impact. When you land, your goal is to not take any extra steps. Pinning your feet to the mat is called sticking the landing. The instant after you land, bring your legs together in a straight stand. Raise your arms in triumph. Smile. You just stuck your landing! (At least you want to act like you did.)

You might be able to complete perfect twists and flips during the postflight of the vault, but none of those skills will matter if you cannot land safely.

THEN AND NOW

Women were not allowed to compete in gymnastics until the 1928 Olympics. Even then, they were limited to synchronized calisthenics, which meant several athletes performing exercises at the same time. Women were finally allowed to compete in individual events in 1952. Women's events today are vault, balance beam, uneven parallel bars, and floor exercise.

Olympic gold medallist Chen Yibing of China poses after a successful landing. Before you reach this pose, there are many important things you must do to stick the landing. But even if you do not stick the landing perfectly, keep your poise and raise your arms in triumph.

SWINGING ON BARS

Three gymnastics events involve bars.

Women compete on the uneven bars. They are two eight-foot-long bars horizontal to the floor. Bars for elite level gymnasts are about 7½ feet and 5 feet off the floor. Men compete on the parallel bars and the high bar. Parallel bars are about 12 feet long, 6½ feet high, and about 1½ feet apart. The high bar is a single bar a little higher than 8 feet off the floor. Gymnasts perform circles and swings in about one minute and complete their routine with a high-flying dismount. Bars exercises require strength, concentration, and split-second timing.

(In parallel bars, men often use both bars at once. In this chapter, we will discuss the use of one bar at a time. The parallel bars are briefly discussed in Tip 19.)

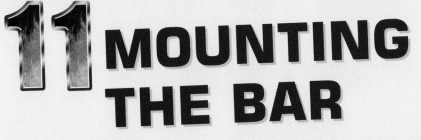

11 MOUNTING THE BAR

You can mount the bars using a springboard. Grasp the bar using any of three grips. Overgrip is palms facing down. You should be able to see the back of your hands. Undergrip is palms facing up. You should be able to see the inside of your wrists. Mixed grip is one hand over and the other under.

THEN AND NOW

In the early 1800s, Friedrich Ludwig Jahn of Germany created the parallel bars. He used a basic ladder and removed its rungs. These wooden bars were stiff. Parallel bars today are made of fiberglass. The bars are bendable, allowing gymnasts to launch higher.

There are three different grips that you can use to grasp the bar. This gymnast is using the overgrip, palms facing down.

The most basic hanging position is the straight hang. In this position, keep your upper body straight and hollow. Hold your legs together and slightly forward. Point your toes to the floor. Other positions, such as tuck and pike, are the same as the body shapes you learned in Tip 1.

12 STARTING MOVEMENTS

The kip is the most common way to get started. Use the glide kip to lift yourself to a support position. Extend your body to a straight hollow position parallel to the floor. Pull your feet in toward the bar. At the same time, pull hard on the bar with your arms straight. You will rise up into a front support on the bar. In this position, your body is straight and tilted at an angle forward of vertical with the bar across your hips. Support your weight with your arms. Keep your elbows locked. Back support is the opposite. Your body is tilted at an angle backward of vertical. The bar is across the back of your thighs. Do not sit on the bar. Support the weight strictly with your arms.

Casting is pushing away from the bar. From front support, pike your body around the bar. Drive your legs backward and up beyond parallel. Keep your arms straight throughout. This is also referred to as a cast pushaway. From this point, you can either return to front support or continue into a handstand. Casting to a handstand requires strong arms and shoulders. Be sure you are able to support yourself in a handstand on the floor before attempting it on the bar.

The tap swing is another way to acquire momentum. From the straight hang, lift your hips back, then kick your toes forward and up. Keep your legs straight. Several tap swings will get you above the bar. You likely learned this motion on a swing. For added control, re-grip the bar for each tap swing.

There are a few ways to get started on the bar. You can use the glide kip to bring yourself to a support position. Casting is pushing away from the bar. The tap swing is another way to gain momentum, and it is similar to the motion you would use on a playground swing.

13 SWINGS AND CIRCLES

A front hip circle takes you forward around the bar. Hold the bar with straight arms in a front support. Push the bar toward your knees, arch your back, then let your upper body fall forward over the bar. You can lurch forward some with your chest as long as you are able to keep your body straight. Your momentum should spin you in a circle around the bar. Keep the bar at thigh level throughout the move. A back hip circle is another basic move. Start in front support. Cast away. Swing your legs forward, under, and up around the bar. Your body should follow. Keep your legs straight and toes pointed.

Giant swings are more difficult. These involve extended arms and straight posture. Legs can be straight or straddled. A backward giant is most common. Use an overhand grip. You can generate long swings to gather momentum by doing taps. Swing in giant revolutions face-first around the bar. Use a reverse grip for the forward giant. Be sure to wear safety straps to keep from losing your grip (see Tip 21).

PRO TIPS AND TRICKS

Nastia Liukin won the 2008 Olympic all-around gold medal for the United States. Liukin's parents were world champion gymnasts in Russia. Liukin says nothing is impossible in gymnastics. "Set daily, monthly, and long-term goals and dreams," she advises. "Don't ever be afraid to dream too big. Nothing is impossible. If you believe in yourself, you can achieve it."

Nastia Liukin performs on the uneven bars during the women's gymnastics team competition at the 2008 Olympic Games in Beijing, China. Olympic champions like Liukin perform difficult skills on the bars, such as giant swings. Before you try the more difficult skills, you want to first perfect the basics.

14 TRANSITIONS

A bar routine is combining swings and circles in a continuous flowing action. Several elements are linked together without pauses. Each change from one skill to the next is called a transition. These changes require different turning elements and grips.

A basic turning element is a pirouette. It is a turn in a handstand. You need to release one hand to place it on the opposite side of the other hand. But both hands must actually change direction. The hand that keeps its position must be reversed from one side of the bar to the other. A general rule is to point your thumb in the direction you are moving. Just as important, be sure to move your body with your hand at the same time. Remember to keep your eyes on the bar!

Move your body with your hand at the same time.

This hand must reverse its position.

Release one hand and place it on the opposite side of the other hand.

One basic turning element during a bar routine is a pirouette. This is done in a handstand. As you do this turning element, make sure to keep your eyes on the bar.

15 THE DISMOUNT

Leaving the bar to finish your routine is called a dismount. Elite gymnasts perform spectacular dismounts out of giants with names like flyaway double tuck and triple back salto (somersault). But before you can do dismounts with multiple flips and twists, you should master a few basics.

The forward roll is an easy dismount. With the bar at your hips in forward support, simply roll forward. Keep your legs in pike. When you arrive at hang position, release the bar and land.

DID YOU KNOW?

Nadia Comaneci of Romania was the first gymnast to receive a perfect score in an Olympic event. At the 1976 Olympic Summer Games in Montreal, Canada, she earned a "10" by the judges in the uneven bars. Amazingly, Comaneci earned six more 10s at the Games.

It is important to learn the basic dismounts from the bar, such as the forward roll, before trying complicated dismounts that are performed by elite level gymnasts. You also want to stick the landing just like in the vault event.

OTHER EVENTS

Women compete in balance beam.

Men compete in pommel horse, rings, and parallel bars. These events demonstrate strength, flexibility, and coordination.

 BALANCE BEAM

The balance beam is 16 feet long, 4 feet high, and just 4 inches wide. Gymnasts perform leaps, turns, and somersaults in a routine lasting up to ninety seconds. Beginners can start by practicing on the floor, then on a beam a few inches off the floor. Once the beam is at full height, a gymnast can mount it using a springboard.

To make the beam feel a bit wider under your feet, swivel them slightly to use the full surface.

The balance beam is just four inches wide, yet the most talented gymnasts can land flips, turns, and somersaults on the beam without falling. Beginners must first master walking on the beam. Swivel your feet to help make the beam feel wider.

Keep your arms out for balance.

When on your hands, keep them flat and wrap your fingers down the sides. Many tricks are similar to those used in floor exercise.

For instance, for a front flip, you simply flip forward and land on the beam. For a switch leap, jump with one foot forward and one behind. Switch your legs in midair before landing. For a back walkover, start tall with your arms up. Lift one leg forward. Point your toes. Lean back into a bridge. Make sure your thumbs touch. Keep your legs split. Push off with your foot. Go straight back and return to standing tall. Reverse it for a front walkover. Perform an aerial walkover by not using your hands.

Use the full length of the beam several times. One movement should flow into the next. Change your rhythm. Make your routine appear to be on the floor, not on a beam.

Lean back into a bridge, then begin by pushing off with your foot.

Point your toes

Both hands on the beam, thumbs touching

This gymnast is performing a back walkover.

The pommel horse is a leather-covered wooden apparatus about five feet long, one foot wide, and four feet above the floor. It has two U-shaped handles called pommels. A gymnast rides the horse by swinging his legs over and around it. He cannot let any part of his body except his hands touch the horse.

You can learn skills using a smaller dome-shaped apparatus called a mushroom. You can walk around the mushroom as you learn to switch hands. You can lift yourself into the air on the mushroom. The trick is to keep your center of gravity over the center of the mushroom.

On the pommel horse, you can perform single-leg and double-leg skills. A standard single-leg skill is scissors. Keep your legs wide apart. Swing each leg alternately to the front and back of the horse. This looks like a pendulum. Keep your weight above your hands. The most common double-leg move is circles. Swing both legs together in circles around the horse. Keep your toes pointed out. You can add variations such as flairs, in which you straddle your legs. Your routine should have a rhythmic flow.

THEN AND NOW

The pommel horse was developed 2,500 years ago. Persian soldiers practiced mounting and dismounting a fake horse for combat on speeding horses in battle. As recently as seventy years ago, the pommel horse in gymnastics had a raised neck and back end in the shape of a real horse. Now the pommel horse is squared off at both ends.

The pommel horse is an event for male gymnasts. The scissors, a single-leg skill pictured here, is done by swinging each leg alternately to the front and back of the horse.

RINGS

Rings is also called still rings. It is an apparatus consisting of two rings that hang by straps from a frame. The rings are about seven inches in diameter and almost ten feet off the floor. Gymnasts hold one ring in each hand and perform tricks while trying to keep the rings from moving.

Rings features two types of skills—swing movements and strength positions. Many swing movements are similar to those used on bars. Moves exclusive to rings include dislocates and Azarians. Ask your coach or instructor how to perform these strength moves.

Holding positions on the rings require a lot of strength. When you begin learning skills on the rings, make sure your coach or instructor is present to help you.

Many of the moves on parallel bars are the same as those described in the bars chapter. To mount the bars, stand between them and jump. Grab one bar in each hand, palms in. Keep your hands even. Don't have one hand in front of the other. Straighten your arms. Do not slump.

Perform bar swings by kicking forward and swinging your body inside the bar. To learn more difficult skills, ask your coach or instructor to teach you.

DID YOU KNOW?

Trampoline is an Olympic sport. It was added to the 2000 Summer Games in Sydney, Australia. Competition takes place on a 14-foot by 7-foot trampoline without a surrounding net. Each athlete jumps to reach enough height, then performs ten leaps without pauses. Tricks include forward and backward somersaults and twists.

The parallel bars is another gymnastics event performed only by boys. However, it involves some of the same skills as the other bar events. When you mount the bars, grab one bar in each hand and keep your hands even.

A list of skills from easiest to most difficult is called progressions. These skills start with basic moves and are grouped by letters, from A to E. You should learn all skills in the A group before you attempt moves in the B or C group.

Gymnasts are ranked by levels from 1 to 10. Beginning gymnasts are Level 1. Your level increases as you master skills from the lettered groups. Junior Elite gymnasts have progressed through all ten levels. Senior Elite is considered Olympic level.

Coaches break down tricks into smaller parts. They use equipment or act as a spotter to ensure your safety. A spotter stands by to hold you for support or to catch you if you fall. Spotting blocks are used to provide support. These blocks are made of high-density foam. For instance, the first time you attempt a back handspring, you should be held by a spotter. When you are ready to try it on your own, you should arch backward over a spotting block.

PRO TIPS AND TRICKS

Shawn Johnson won the 2008 Olympic gold medal in the balance beam. Johnson admits that she was nervous before the event. "I don't think I've ever not gotten nervous," she says. "When you work so hard for one special day or routine, you want to perform it better than you ever have. We always say at our gym, 'If you lose the nerves, you lose the sport.'"

There are ten levels in gymnastics and advancing to each skill level is called progression. It takes a lot of time to perfect each skill and technique. Frequently, coaches will break down tricks into smaller parts to make them easier. They also act as spotters and use safety equipment to help you learn. These two coaches help a young gymnast on the vault.

PREPARING TO COMPETE

Gymnastics can be a world of fun,

especially if you prepare wisely. Here are some more tips to give you an extra edge.

 **GEAR**

Your gym should have some basic supplies. For events on the bars, you can apply powdered chalk to your hands. This is called "chalking up." The chalk absorbs moisture and reduces friction. The chalk is called "mag" for magnesium carbonate. Just don't rely on the chalk. Beginning gymnasts panic when they notice their chalk wearing off.

Dowel grips or handguards protect your palms from blisters. They strap over your fingers and fasten around your wrist with Velcro or buckles. Safety straps wrap in a loop around the bar. Put a hand through each loop,

PRO TIPS AND TRICKS

Among America's first great male gymnasts was Kurt Thomas. He won the gold medal in floor exercise at the 1978 World Championships and then several more international medals. Kurt's success came from learning to handle pressure. "Ninety percent of gymnastics is the mental ability to perform when the time comes," Thomas says.

spin your hand to tighten the strap around your wrist, and grab the bar. When you are very high, you can wear a safety belt around your waist.

Gymnasts find creative ways to protect their hands. Boys wear gardening gloves. Girls wear socks. Olympic gymnast Mary Lou Retton put Vaseline and vitamin E on her hands at night and wore socks over her hands as she slept to soften her calluses.

Young gymnasts wearing safety guards put chalk, or "mag," on their hands. Gymnasts use this chalk to help keep their grip during training and competitions.

22 NUTRITION

To be an elite athlete, you must eat properly. First, know the five food groups. They are grains, vegetables, fruits, dairy products, and meat and fish. For a balanced diet, eat from all of these groups. Protein from meat, nuts, and dairy products, such as milk and eggs, help build muscles. Grains from potatoes, bread, and cereal provide long-term energy. Fruits give you an energy burst. It is important to eat at the right time. Never skip breakfast. Eat a sandwich or some pasta a few hours before practice. Eat a piece of fruit during practice. Be sure to drink plenty of water!

All those flips, spins, twists, and tumbles will leave even the most conditioned gymnast worn out. It is important to eat properly and drink plenty of water.

THEN AND NOW

Top women gymnasts once were much older than they are today. Agnes Keleti of Hungary was thirty-five years old when she won three gold medals at the 1956 Olympics. Larissa Latynina of the Soviet Union was twenty-nine when she won six medals at the 1964 Games. Compare that to the 2008 Olympics. All-around winner Nastia Liukin of the United States was eighteen years old. American Shawn Johnson and China's Yang Yilin, who finished second and third, were both sixteen.

Gymnastics requires agility. This is your ability to change your body's position. To form body shapes, you need to be flexible. You want to spend plenty of time stretching. This helps prevent muscles and ligaments from tearing. First, you need to get your heart pumping and blood flowing. Warm up with some jumping jacks or a light jog around the gym. Now you are ready to stretch. Carefully roll your head around to stretch your neck. Extend your arms to the sides and make circles. Put your hands on your hips. Lean forward, backward, and side to side. Take a wide stance. Reach down and touch the floor. Repeat this several times.

Put your legs together and do the same stretch. If you are able, do the splits. Assume the bridge position (see Tip 1).

Flexibility is important in gymnastics, and stretching will help improve your flexibility. But stretching before training and competition is important to avoid injury, too.

24 STRENGTH TRAINING

Gymnastics requires strength. The best way to get stronger is by strength training. Be sure to ask your coach or instructor whether you are old enough to begin strength training. When you start, always use proper form. Here are four basic strength moves that work your major muscle groups.

1. **Push-ups**—Place your hands on the floor shoulder-width apart with your feet together behind you. Keep your body straight. Push up equally with both arms, then carefully lower yourself back down.

2. **Pull-ups**—Hang from a bar with your body straight. Lift your chin up past the bar. You should do overhand and underhand pull-ups.

3. **Lunges**—Stand with your knees slightly bent. Step forward and lower your body until your forward thigh is parallel to the floor. Return to the starting position. Keep your upper body upright.

4. **Crunches**—Lay on your back on the floor. Lift your thighs straight up and bend your knees at a right angle. Hold your hands behind your head. Carefully lift up a few inches. Exhale. Keep your stomach muscles tight and your back pressed into the floor.

There are some basic strength training drills you can do that require no equipment. Push-ups are a great way to strengthen your upper body.

Most other sports have seasons. Gymnastics is a year-round sport. When you aren't practicing for your next competition, you want to stay fit. Stamina is your ability to keep going. You can increase your stamina with aerobic exercise. Aerobics uses oxygen. By exercising at a steady pace, you strengthen your heart and lungs.

There are many forms of aerobics you can do. Play basketball or tennis for an hour. Ride a bike for forty minutes. Jog for thirty minutes. Swim without stopping for twenty minutes. You can even take an aerobics class. Any activity that requires deep breathing for at least twenty minutes will increase your stamina. Just keep moving and have fun!

DID YOU KNOW?

Rhythmic gymnastics is another form of the sport. It can be performed by individuals or as many as six teammates at once. Competitors do tricks with balls, clubs, hoops, and ribbons. Judges award points for tumbling moves, handling of the equipment, and artistic effort. In 1984, rhythmic gymnastics became an Olympic sport.

Practice your skills, work hard, and dream big, and someday you could be wearing a medal at the Olympic Games.

GLOSSARY

★**absorb**—To soften the force of a weight.

★**accelerate**—To move or go faster. Speed up.

★**aerial**—Being in the air.

★**apparatus**—One or more instruments, tools, or other pieces of equipment.

★**center of gravity**—The point around which your body rotates.

★**choreographed**—Put together in a group or list.

★**dismount**—To get off something that is in the air.

★**elite**—The highest in class or best of a group.

★**leading leg**—The leg that is in front of or forward of the other.

★**momentum**—The force or speed of movement.

★**pivots**—Spins or other rotations, usually on the balls of the feet.

★**propel**—To shoot forward through the air with force.

★**trailing leg**—The leg that is behind or backward of the other.

★**tumbling**—Performing acrobatic moves on a mat.

★**vertical**—Straight up and down. Perpendicular to the floor.

FURTHER READING

Books

Brown, Heather. *How to Improve at Gymnastics.* New York: Crabtree Publishing Co., 2009.

Challen, Paul. *Flip It Gymnastics*. New York: Crabtree Publishing Co., 2010.

Jones, Jen. *Gymnastics Competitions: On Your Way to Victory*. Mankato, Minn.: Capstone Press, 2007.

McIntosh, J. S. *Gymnastics*. Broomall, Pa.: Mason Crest Publishers, 2011.

Page, Jason. *Gymnastics Events*. New York: Crabtree Publishing Co., 2008.

Schlegel, Elfi and Claire Ross Dunn. *The Gymnastics Book: The Young Performer's Guide to Gymnastics*. Buffalo, N.Y.: Firefly Books, 2001.

Internet Addresses

The Drills and Skills Page: Gymnastics Technique and Training
<http://www.drillsandskills.com/>

Gymnastics Revolution: Gymnastics Interactive
<http://www.gymnasticsrevolution.com/GymInteractive-Intro.htm>

USA Gymnastics
<http://www.usa-gymnastics.org/pages/index.html>

INDEX